PEOPLE LEAVE, FEELINGS STAY

People Leave, Feelings Stay

A collection of poems about breakups, healing, and the search for romantic love.

L. GERARD

Lauren R. Bobersky

First paperback edition April 2024

Book design by Lauren R. Bobersky

ISBN 979-8-2183980-6-4 (paperback)
ISBN 979-8-2183980-7-1 (ebook)

www.lgerardpoet.com

For my family.

Table of Contents

Author's Note

This is a breakup book.

Breakups are sad and also fascinating. I noticed something strange about my artistic life, that it is easier to create when I am some sort of heartbroken. My theory about this is that when we are sad, we are in desperate need for an outlet. We need the pain to leave our minds and our bodies, we just need it to go away because the state of perceived permanence is unbearable. We also need the pain to mean something, because it would be too tragic if we were feeling such sorrow and had nothing to show for it.

Enter art. Enter feeling connected, and a respite that only comes when you take the energy of sorrow and make it into something outside of yourself. Something tangible.

When we are happy though, we want it to stay. Unlike the sadness that we are convinced is everlasting, happiness brings a hyper-awareness of the ephemeral. And we fight all we can to keep it. As if we could. Even though this battle often distracts us from simply enjoying and being, it feels righteous and important. It is hard to walk away from.

We are going to feel so much during our remaining days in this version of the universe. And truthfully, both violently gripping to our feelings or desperately trying to throw them away doesn't work. It is a package deal, and the only way to fully absorb the good and get through the bad is simply to let yourself feel them and honor them when they are there.

The emotional experience is not linear, and some love stories are very short. And some don't actually end if we are being honest with ourselves. It is not always easy to remember, but it is a privilege to miss someone. I am grateful for the pain in this book. And I am grateful for the hope in this book. Thank you for letting me share these words with you.

I.

There are moments, memories, even days that you simply exist through. They seem inconsequential and mundane, as most of our days do. There is a special beauty to this ordinary. A right turn on the sidewalk, staying for one more drink, sitting on that park bench. Upon reflection you look back to what was at the time almost a thoughtless experience and realize it was important. A crucial component to one of your life's befores and afters. The true indication that these moments were life-changing only reveals itself as time passes. The correlations come to light and you pinpoint what once was just another day as a critical plot point of your life.

The night we fell in love was, without any question and with all of the weight of unabashed certainty, not like this. I was so young and so hopeful and so just coming into who I wanted to be. As soon as my eyes met yours as you walked toward me, my body was absolutely electric with the awareness that everything had changed. Was changing. That entire night – still, heartbreakingly and honestly the best of my life – each second that passed came with acute awareness that it was of life-altering importance. Consciousness in real time that my present is becoming a precious memory. It is almost shocking that the weight of it all didn't crush me – but again, I was young and in awe of you and already flying.

London

My face smiled –
A panic response or muscle memory
Unclear and sad either way

And from what I can recall
I said the right things
If in this situation, there ever are any right things to say

I shook her hand
Hugged you –
Something that took so many hours
Of tears and physical pain
To accept would never happen again

And I barely remember it moments later
Shock does strange things to the body
And the body remembers
Which creates a uniquely confusing state
But the entire time my heart
It was screaming

I still write poetry about you.

Anywhere

Another one last night – a dream
The dream, different but also always the same
Forgiveness and reconciliation
We were together again
And we always kiss and god you're such a good kisser

It's been years and I'm still dreaming somehow
I was learning though, slowly
Finally aware even in my subconscious state
This is a dream and its lifespan is a moment
Dejected and resigned to its ephemerality

Yet when you kiss me I enjoy it all the same
I am warm and safe and infinite all the same
So desperate for absolution in any realm, really

But last night I got the better of myself
A laughable battle between denial and repair
I looked you in the eyes and said
"This isn't even a dream, this is real"
And all of me believed it

So I woke up with a punched gut
And the darkness that is the shadow of your lips
That never actually left

II.

I'm walking alone on the sidewalk on my way home. Tonight was another big city night with big love and big laughs and friends and all the stuff that is well and good and fine. And suddenly, I have the audacity to start singing – out loud – the song that I always thought would be our first dance. At our wedding I used to know would happen someday with the conviction one can only have when in love for the first time.

Why do I still give so much power to what could have been after so many years of over? How would you react to me doing this, still? How would I want you to? It would be too tragic, if you feel the same way and we are in the same city (yet so far apart) and we are so broken – too broken – to fix each other's hearts. I need you to be happy. And I need you to stay where you are, which I imagine now is apathy. I cannot have you drift to this harrowing place like I do. I will sing alone, because I simply cannot wish this persistent pain on you.

Prospect Park

You said the game was three words
And you thought about mine
And that means you thought about me –
When I wasn't there

And I could have died right then
Suffocated from clutching this idea of you thinking of me
My name in that gorgeous head of yours
So tight to my chest that I puncture my lungs
My decomposing body smiling at the arbitrary violence
My heart had already exploded anyway after our knees touched
Stupidly happy, a lost cause
I already couldn't breath

With big eyes and somehow zero expectations
I looked at you and listened
Whatever you said would be the best thing I ever heard so
Please just keep talking
The first two words, you said, were
Infectious and addictive
I said you make me sound like a disease, you laugh
Because it's so obvious to you that you're complimenting me

It's actually dangerous, you say
That's the third word, you say
Because it is dangerous how infectious I am
And how you already feel addicted to me

And we have never kissed
And already hugged goodbye
And I never got to ask
Why our connection was so unsafe for you

July

We experience time
In that restrictive linear way
Sure, sometimes our minds
Try to travel to the past
Or pretend we can play the future
But we are here, and only here
It's just a matter of if we are paying attention

You walked into the room, though
And my body knew something
My mind couldn't yet
A soul remembering
Stood its ground and calmly
Assured my conscious to simply let the time pass

The truth always reveals itself
And your bottom lip has somehow
Always been a guidepost of safety for me
And our bodies not touching has somehow
Always been a situation to be addressed

Managing to find infinity
In a story that is just starting
And also feels like it has already happened
The ending's existence now inconsequential
Longevity useless since it is so clearly written
The beauty that is here
And the honor of stroking your back
They are permanent

III.

I am in a cab home after a night out. There were friends from different parts of my life and everyone was happy to see me. I was myself and I asked good questions and I heard the same compliments and part of me was present and grateful. I was in awe of how amazing people are, but another part of me felt like everything is on repeat and nothing is original. Or at least, nothing possibly can be again until I actually give my heart again to someone. The whole thing. The whole fucking thing. I've done all this work that everyone says you're supposed to. I actually wake up in the morning now somewhat grateful to be alive and yet everything is the same. Until it isn't because you now have that feeling. Feeling the absolute resolution that everything in your life is forever changed because someone that didn't exist yesterday will now, because of today, exist forever.

And for a short while you can ignore the other truth that everything ends. So for now, the choice is denial. You indulge in the possibility, the vast horizon that is unadulterated potential, and you feel the closest you ever will to what forever actually means. And then you're torn because you want to pause and just be with this person who is a human, like you, but somehow also more pure than anything on this earth could be. But you also can't wait to go to sleep just to wake up and experience tomorrow with them. But tomorrow with them is also one day closer to the day someone dies or it's over anyway and you find yourself gathering material for a eulogy you know is going to kill you.

Curved Blade

It may be pompous and sick in the head
But even smug villains are sometimes right
And that's even harder to deal with isn't it

You still hear my heartbeat
And that song will never be just yours
You turned me evil and ugly and you thought that would help

But you hear your nickname in my voice
And *I love you* simply hasn't felt the same
So caught up blaming my impulsiveness for killing us
You missed that it's your pride with blood stained hands

Pulse

Could have been you
But it wasn't
Actually it could not have been you –
That gait of yours
It's my heartbeat

No, I can't produce the rhythm
Simply an integration of my existence
Lifeblood

And the pacemaker
Of distraction and nearly new love
Almost laughable
How negligent the surgery was
No one even washed their hands

Every day on the sidewalk
Walking just because my legs move
Knowing if it was actually you
Everything would stop

IV.

I was terrified of biking. Sometime between the invincibility of adolescence and learning that people you love can die (is this what getting older is?) I became fearful of both driving and biking. Walking or running were the only dependable ways of getting anywhere because my body was the only thing I had to control. I lived in a big city and it is rational to fear biking, anyhow. I was in no rush to change. But now I have. Which is a nice reminder that I am allowed to. I wear my helmet and I bike all of the time and it gets me places faster and there is a freedom of going downhill that reminds me of the irreproachable freedom of being a child and not knowing any better.

And the first time, which was before now, I was so scared. Yes I was terrified, but you were there and said I would be fine and at that point it was dangerous, the degree to which I'd believe anything you said to me. I insisted you ride in front of me because I had no idea how to get where we were going, but I also knew the only place I wanted to go was where you were. And humor through a heartbreaking memory is the imprinted image in my mind of your face looking back at me. Your big eyes were somehow even brighter and bigger and you wanted to make me smile and make sure I was alright. The fact that this certainly made the situation deeply more dangerous for you I suppose is a cruel foreshadowing that we never notice when we are too busy falling in love.

Rue Saint-Honoré

Our interactions, the time between them has been too long
Or maybe it has just felt like perpetuity
Since somehow I'm already so dependent on you
Struggling to decipher if we are decidedly past tense

I was so sure
The electricity was so instantaneous
Its entrance could not even be noticed
Because it was already the universe of energy between us

I walked right into it
Off the edge, I cannot even pretend I didn't know better
You cracked me open
And I loved that I could still feel
This is special and good
And that can be present tense
Even if only in my memory

We were a lovely light
I could see things now
But when you could finally see yourself
You wanted to close your eyes
I'm not too much
You're not enough yet

I was so sure
You'd be another story
I wanted you anyway
For as many seconds as I could have you
My heart hadn't welcomed guests in so long
And you were never a stranger
We just had not overlapped yet

Sackett Street

I woke up with puffy eyes
A friendly reminder of retention
That last night I tried to release
So much of the sad

A bit sick but I do feel some relief
Not to recognize myself
Seeing you threw me out of orbit
Time travel and disorientation

A bit sick but I do feel some fondness
My swollen skin temporary evidence
That you still exist at all
And once upon a time you touched me

The tragedy of so much ending
My lap was your head's second home
We made a song about the moon
Our default assumption was forever

I said to you so many times
I couldn't imagine life without you
You said *luckily, you don't have to*
With the naïveté of thinking I could let myself keep you

V.

I am not sure if time ever passed slower than those days after we met and I was waiting to hear from you. What a cruel counterbalance to the night we met, and how those hours of evening to early morning simply and instantly dissolved. The absolute thrill of possibility was a beautiful place to live. I kept replaying our goodbye, which even after five hours felt staggering and too soon. You turned back and waved to me from the sidewalk as my car drove away, and for the first time in what might as well have been forever I was hopeful again. The urge to periodically scream *are you real* that night was simply no rival for the fire that burned that impulse to the ground – indisputably knowing that you are good. You just are.

I gave you my phone number, but something undeniable in my bones told me that there is a version of this universe in which I also give you my life. And you were still a stranger after all, weren't you? To me an insignificant detail, because my weary and jaded and broken semblance of a belief in love finally was able to stand up and see a gorgeous sunrise of a new beginning.

House Party

Deep breath, shallow reset
Starting over from something that did not start at all
A conscious, well practiced detachment
Trauma making itself useful

Options are simply limited
When possibility becomes a shadow
I could wonder if self-fulfilling prophecy is involved
But I am tired and my spirit hurts

I will believe in love tomorrow
Throw away all the empty cans and clean the sticky floor
Until then I'll drink my toxin of doubt
Sorrow-bodied and goes down so easily, every time

Pool Party

I felt it
The magic, I know
It was there
We sparkled, bliss
In the sunlight
I was so warm

We laid on the ground
Yet I was flying
It was there
My mouth hurt
How you looked at me
Sore jaw, smiling wide
This must be what
My mother used to call
"Good pain"

I was me, you were you
It was there, we were there
Together, the energy
They teach you
In school, but this
This is what it means –
A chemical reaction

Magic is real
I will die, believing
That to be true
We were real
But for whatever
Reason, this was
Ephemeral, too short
And seasonal

You now have context
And I am not me,
Not to you, now
Between awe of
Reunion, and now
The beginning has
Transformed, entirely
I ache through it
Since now it is the
Beginning of the end

VI.

You were like going underwater into the freezing cold and being short of breath. And it was scary. It was scary but it was also good and important because I forgot how much of a gift it is to breathe. And the fear and discomfort is such a small and silly cost for the beauty of remembering. It was what I needed. The smallest fraction of hours in an entire lifetime brought me what I needed. For you, though, I won't ever know because our moment, for whatever reason, was not adequate to bring us together again.

But *wants*. That is where things get dangerous. That's when I want to remain underwater and I don't realize until it is too late that the consequence of that is drowning.

I want another kiss. Then another, then another. I want to know which side of the bed would be yours. I want to know the feeling of my lips on your shoulder blades as I kiss them while you're sleeping. I want to know what we would fight about. And what we wouldn't fight about. I want to know where you would touch me to let me know you're there. I want to know where we would be when I tell you I love you for the first time.

Senescence

My heart is a geriatric
You aged it
Make no mistake, it is not doing well for its age
Can barely walk or take care of itself
There are discussions of hospice.

We never wanted to wish time away –
My heart, my mind, and me,
The three of us made an agreement not to do that,
Life is precious and whatnot.

But alas
Extenuating circumstances arose
And staying young, staying here
Too broken, not possible
An absolutely unsustainable strategy
A crippling burden on the trio.

So instead I violently hurled us into the future
Now elderly and crotchety
So impatient with a new someone else's pulse
But alive for now
At least in the literal sense.

Traffic

Sometimes we get more
But so often we don't
Hope is tricky
Hard to come by in the first place
And then the production that is navigating the proper amount
Exhausting

All too often you realize you indulged in too much
It is not a matter of degree
Too much is too much
Which is crushed
Again

I wonder through my staggered breaths and wet eyes
Why I bothered at all
Apathy has never seemed sexier
And it works
A flickering flame of reprieve

Until the spark fades and you realize
You've been truly alone the entire time
And you don't remember as much
And not paying attention to your life makes you feel less human
And what you did to stay alive
Seemingly annihilates you even more

So the cycle continues
Another walk into the street with my eyes closed
But if I don't move I will just stay here
Which has become so unbearable
I can almost believe
It might be different this time

VII.

Sometimes when I'm walking alone in the morning and the sun hits my skin just right, or I'm upstate and it is dark and I can see the stars, I let myself indulge. I play every remaining memory of that first night. Of us. These memories dissolve with time, and we all know how memories become works of fiction sooner than we would like to admit. But if something feels real, after all of this time, I'm not sure how much it matters in the end.

We were in the basement of the bar, which in that moment of my life was the coolest place I'd ever been to simply because you took me there. We were sitting next to each other and our legs were touching and my heart was on fire. We befriended a couple – one from Cairo, one from Paris. They met randomly on the other side of the world, yet somehow my knee pressing against yours felt more miraculous.

We told them that we had been together for a year and a half, and we were so natural and comfortable and somehow already so in love they believed it. I even almost did. What a cruel and funny choice, that amount of time specifically, because the reality of our time together was barely much longer than that. A callous co-incidence, sure, but it pales in comparison to the serendipity that brought us together. And the truth is, that although in a very certain context, we fit within that time frame, the privilege of being loved by you has taught me what forever actually means.

Our City

I left again
Enough time has passed
The spectators are no longer suspicious
Almost undetectable
Though haphazard and pathetic at best
My decisions and desperation
To construct my life, simply
So you weren't everywhere

Once acceptable, since
There is a grace period
Please help me with this, thank you
If our pain makes sense to other people
We can deteriorate shame-free
This ends eventually, though
How long can one expect other people
To carry something so heavy anyway

So the truth is now mine and mine alone
Grossly oppressive and boring
But truth gets to be whatever it wants
Its power inherent and irrefutable in its existence
Nothing to be done
A whisper or a scream
I hear it −

I'm here because you're not.

Home

I haven't been writing recently
Which typically means that I am either really happy
or depressed
All too often the answer is both

There is a certain threshold that cannot truly be defined
But involves heartbreak of different flavors
and pain finding unique places to put holes in your spirit
that you weren't sure even existed until they were compromised

When it is reached, over time
Joy no longer exists in its own; two for the price of one
Every moment of big smiles and absolutely full heart
comes with a side of grief or an awareness that all of this will
go away
or simply a reminder that, no, they aren't here anymore

I've tried to stop having expectations
for all things – people (especially), how my life will go, how my
life won't go
It didn't serve me and was a self created slap in the face about
the things I cannot control
But when something is good for you and the entire system isn't
It's a constant practice to unlearn so much sometimes
and we are only human after all

And the cumulative pressure and simple expenditure of energy
really adds up
The pressure valve can burst right along with my self-awareness
and ability to be present
and my peace of mind and my knowledge that how they deal
with their pain is not about me
and how far I have come with my own pain

I recognize myself less so I also just look in the mirror less
And the delicious taste of self-indulgent pity and the solace of
the black hole of my bed
become dangerously close to a state of potential permanence
And it happens so fast and all too quickly
that one of the many people I am grieving is myself

And these things take time
And I choose to give myself grace
People die or they leave anyway and I know now that when they
do that feelings stay
And I choose to stop creating my own problems
When I know all too well that life does just fine with that
without the help of my own violent hand or twisted mind

And this pain that I carry
Doesn't always need to make me heavier
It does at first and it always will at first
and it has been fifteen years and I still can't hear that song

But I feel this way because oh my god I feel this way
I feel
Everything
I love oh so hard so deep so much and that is why I am alive
And it is how I remember in the dark and scary places that I'm
not actually dying
And I get to choose to live.

VIII.

I'm still going to hold onto it. Not any of the meticulously curated plot lines, like the one where I look over at you on the front porch while drinking tea and see you reading a book and my heart still swells in adoration after so many years. It seems as though they are not going to happen. Or more directly, I know I will never have you. But my heart and mind have started to take me to these places and that has not happened since before (him).

Barely knowing you, and already feeling like I simply cannot be close enough to you, this in itself is a gift. I choose for this to further open my heart. I refuse to close. And this is part of our story, however short it may be, and I am so on board. In any case, meeting you was an exceptional part of mine and it is the way it is supposed to be.

Fall

The leaves have changed
Are changing
You cannot look at the trees without noticing

And I want to be aware of it
It's the natural state of things
Why would I want to dismiss such transformation?

I owe it to myself
Dare I say to those I love
Those that love me

To see the colors
Sit in the ephemerality that is everything
Honor the courage it can take
To simply pay attention

The world is in motion
I am becoming myself

Open Nerve

It didn't have to be you
I don't think it could have been anyone
But the moments happened
And moments are multi-talented
They can create a bright light of now
Or create an antagonistic permanence
That makes your heart ache and your hope dissolve

And for whatever random reason
Or force of nature
Or kind coincidence
It was you
And my moments and your moments
Irrevocably became eternally ours

I was cold and dressed up
And the party was ending
But you came outside
And everything else was over
Because it was concrete and clear
Everything else was simply the route to our beginning

And even though I ended it
And severed what might as well have been my limbs
That feeling of infinity
Is integrated into my forever emotional landscape

And the crater I scraped into my own heart
Is a black hole I'm still lost in sometimes
But it's a small price of admission
For the memory of your lips on my collarbone
And watching you sleep
And believing in magic

Acknowledgements

Thank you to my mother, who during a phone call a few weeks ago asked me, "How is your second book coming?"

Thank you to my family. You believe I am exceptional, and that makes me want to be. I love and like you endlessly.

Thank you to my friends who actually are my family. We cannot hold our shattered hearts by ourselves. Everything is lighter with the delight you bring to my life.

Thank you to anyone that has ever read a piece of my work.

And, finally, something taken from the Acknowledgements of my first book; it is as true and important to say as before: If you are someone that has loved me, or that I have loved, then I am grateful for you and this book would not exist without you. My life is abundant with care, and I am grateful for this every day. The way I aim to live my life is so you already know who you are. Thank you.

About the Author

L. Gerard is the pen name of author Lauren Rachel Bobersky. She uses this pen name in honor of her father Gerard Bobersky, who died in 2006. She lives in Austin with her cat, Finn.

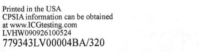

9 798218 398064